CTRL ALT DELETE

Democracy in Reboot

Dennis Ondrejka

Ctrl Alt Delete: Democracy in Reboot

Copyright © 2021 Dennis Ondrejka. All rights reserved. No part of this book may be reproduced or retransmitted in any form or by any means without the written permission of the publisher.

Published by Wheatmark®
2030 East Speedway Boulevard, Suite 106
Tucson, Arizona 85719 USA
www.wheatmark.com

ISBN: 978-1-62787-889-0 (paperback)
ISBN: 978-1-62787-890-6 (ebook)
LCCN: 2021909526

Bulk ordering discounts are available through Wheatmark, Inc. For more information, email orders@wheatmark.com or call 1-888-934-0888.

Table of Contents

Recognition and Thanks	v
Prelude	vii
Chapter 1: Awakening	1
Chapter 2: Historical Democracy: Actions and Failures in the United States	25
Chapter 3: Recent Democracy Failures	31
Chapter 4: Congress in Reboot	41
Chapter 5: Executive in Reboot	49
Chapter 6: Supreme and Federal Courts in Reboot	55
Chapter 7: State Criminal System in Reboot	61
Chapter 8: First Amendment in Reboot (Free Speech, Social Media Issues, and Religious Freedom in Particular)	67
Chapter 9: Education in Reboot	77
Chapter 10: Taxation in Reboot	83

Conclusion	89
Appendix I	91
Appendix II	117

Recognition and Thanks

My initial idea was to produce a book that was mostly blank, giving room for other ideas. I want to thank Janet Lorimer for her support and dedication in assisting me in revising and increasing the depth of this content to make it a real book. Janet has been a tremendous support in editing and advising the entire process.

Prelude

If I were to ask you to rate our United States democracy over the past 250 years on a scale from 1 to 10, with 1 being disgust and 10 being wonderful, what number would you pick?

Go ahead and pick a number and write it here: _____.

I am currently only at a 2, and that is why I need to do something. I see a 2 as disgust with a tiny piece of hope. I want to hit control alt delete on the entire process because I think it's time for dramatic change. A few years ago, I would have given it a 7 or 8, thinking we just needed to work on some issues. I ignored all the harmful things we did as a country while insisting we were the best democratic nation on earth.

Who is Dennis Ondrejka? Well, that is a good question without a good answer. I am nothing special and have no agenda greater than creating awareness in Americans regarding what is and what could be in our Constitution and amendments. I believe there are inherent errors and holes in a document that was written by aristocratic white men during a time of slavery, occupying only thirteen states, suffering recent wounds from a war with Great Britain, needing independence, and fearing a powerful government.

We have had amendments over the years, but even this is such a cumbersome issue that to make additional amendments is very challenging. I find it quite interesting how most Americans have a strong faith in the way the Constitution and amendments are meant to serve our fellow citizens, *and yet* they know so little about what is really in this document. I believe we have created an illusion and false narrative regarding its content and original meaning.

When I hear someone say he or she is a "Constitutionalist," I get very nervous as to what that means—especially when he or she is a Supreme Court justice. One example would be for them to support the Second Amendment and its original meaning. The phrase "a well-regulated Militia, being necessary to the security of a Free State" is a very interesting idea. Does that mean we should have a militia ready to control the federal government to protect states' rights? Or, is this what we might call the National Guard, which is in place and regulated by the states and connected to the federal army's agendas as well? The National Guard is called up by state governors and also joins the US Army to fight in international military operations. I was a part of this organization and knew that I had a double allegiance, but what does the Second Amendment mean by its wording? I hope we all can think about such things as we move through this book.

The chapter headings are primarily constructed around certain topics. This should get everyone started. I want this book to continue to grow using reader comments and ideas for change. You will be referred to a blog where you can send your ideas to me for the next version of this book. When you respond, state the chapter or topic to which you are responding. Place the rationale for the change in *italics* right after your recommendation.

Chapters 4 through 10 will begin with what I think needs change related to that topic. My rationale for the change is set in *italic print*. Join in, continue the conversation, and send your ideas to this blog: ctrl-alt-delete.us. I am learning more and more as I write this book, and now I am beginning to awaken. I hope the same is true for you. Please continue the dialogue on the blog so I can explore more ideas of what we can do for our democracy. Thank you for joining me on this journey.

CHAPTER 1

Awakening

I believe former president Trump helped me realize that what we have is democratic Swiss cheese. He did not help me understand how to deepen my acceptance of what we have but rather showed me the depth of weaknesses and cracks in the current democracy as I thought I knew it. In fact, I believe I was living in some type of bubble that was only beginning to open from time to time.

You may be sick of what is showing up in our democracy and want to hit reboot or even explore a revolt. My personal bias is that democracy in America needs more than a backspace or using an insert key to offer minor adjustments. I believe we need to slam on the brakes and make dramatic changes. The problem with doing this type of major change is related to the challenging process required for constitutional change.

Article V of the Constitution only provides two processes for such amendments to occur. One is by a two-thirds affirmative vote by both houses, and the second is by a three-fourths majority of all states approving such action. That would mean thirty-eight states agreeing to change the Constitution. However, I am in good company when it comes to believing Constitutional changes are necessary. Mr. Jefferson's letter to Samuel Kercheval, July 12, 1816, on the *Subject of Convention,* is a powerful wake-up call to have regular Constitutional reform. *"Some people look at the constitution with sanctimonious reverence, and deem them, like the ark of the covenant, too sacred to be touched.... I am certainly not an advocate for frequent and untried changes in laws and constitution. But I know that laws and institutions must go hand in hand with the progress of the human mind. As that [society] becomes more developed, more enlightened, as new discoveries are made, new truths discovered and manners and opinions change, with the change of circumstances, institutions must advance also to keep pace with the times. We might as well require a man to wear still the coat which fitted him when a boy, as [to require] civilized society to remain ever under the regimen of their barbarous ancestors"* (https://www.loc.gov/resource/rbc0001.2021madison38216/?sp=1&r=-1.693,0.114,4.386,1.752,0, p. 8).

I believe we are now headed for such a change.

We have a host of perspectives regarding the sanctity of the current Constitution and amendments. If we explored all the variations, we might see a dramatic dichotomy in thought. My current dilemma is how the idea of a democracy in reboot might be seen from so many perspectives.

Those who stormed the US Capitol on January 6, 2021, were ready to push our current democracy over a cliff because they followed a narrative created by false beliefs, lies, and propaganda. My words describing that narrative are highly controversial, as tens of millions of Americans believe the conspiracy falsehoods to be true. I call it a lie, and many would call this the truth exposing the "deep state."

More than half of the citizens of the United States would agree with me and denounce the attack on the Capitol building. Regardless of my beliefs, millions believe the election was stolen and are still looking for a resolution to that idea. How can such dichotomy be reconciled by changing our Constitution? That is my struggle in writing this book, but I must try.

Do we reboot democracy regardless of how we see the issues, or do we need to be more honest and forgiving about what our history tells us? This is a challenging idea for change because it is coming from so many different perspectives. I do not believe the stolen election story, so the angle that drives me comes from constant failures of living up to the Constitution's intent or lack of clarity in its wording. If you notice a bias in this book, that is it.

I don't believe the storming of the US Capitol was an attempt to improve our current democracy. I see it as an attempt to destroy foundational democratic principles in which the people get to vote for a president after which the Electoral College casts its votes based on the people's choice. I may not like this process, but it is the current Constitutional approach to electing a president and vice president.

A destructive revolt does not mean you are concerned about democracy. You might believe something is not true, but you have no right in this country to destroy and kill for that belief, and I am not supporting such an action. Destructive revolts could mean you do not care about democracy in the least or maybe it is your goal to change what is. It does mean that democracy has serious issues that need cleansing.

I am struggling with how we can have rules and a Constitution, but we do not hold people accountable for such antidemocratic actions as promoting conspiracy theories that end in violence or insurrection.

Senators and representatives who were engaged at some level with the rioters on January 6, 2021, have not yet been held to account under Amendment 14, Section 3. Failure to preserve what is valued in our Constitution is a concern to me and makes me wonder if the rules are strong enough or clear enough to uphold.

America has turned democracy into a skeleton of what I—and maybe you—thought it was.

Is the Constitution impossible to follow? Is it a bad idea? How have we been able to experience so many failures of democracy during our American history under a document that would appear to prevent such abuses?

I have smashed into a wall of concern as to what should happen next. I realize the first step is to know what our Constitution and amendments state. I have placed them in Appendices I and II at the end of this book for your review. I have been reading and reviewing these documents and listening to the news on how democracy is working for today's citizens, and I am very concerned and angry regarding how it fails those it was meant to protect.

Is it possible that congressional leaders and the president can create an environment where taking the oath to uphold the Constitution has no meaning? Can I take an oath to uphold the Constitution and then violate that oath without any consequences? Maybe taking an oath does not mean what I thought it meant. However, I know what it should mean!

You might believe our freedom of speech allows us to say anything at any time without any consequence of what that speech generates. Is that what the Constitution allows me to do? Are we in an era where we believe in a nonfactual narrative, and those in power will keep the falsehood alive in a way that could uproot many aspects of the Constitution? Is this freedom of speech?

I have learned how large groups of people can be persuaded to believe an untruth if it is told repeatedly. Another current persuasion technique is to create a false narrative and then use that falsehood to propagate additional false ideas. In my past academic studies, I had never heard of these persuasion methods. Still, it seems to be very effective in our recent history.

There are several layers of the January 6 insurrectionist group: some are angry, some are actively protesting, and others are ready to kill and take over the government. All these approaches are crashing into each other. I don't believe this is freedom of speech and that it is expressly prohibited under the First Amendment as well as being criminal.

Another group ties the idea of disenfranchisement to a historical civil war and/or deep-seated privilege. This group does not see how there is privilege in just being "white." I understand how they are in this mindset, but I also know it is privilege. It is privilege to not be in a host of minority groups throughout American history.

In my own growth, I continue to see new and shocking examples of economic and racial bias. The most recent painful expressions of implicit bias are in police violence toward African American citizens and in *anti-voting right bills* spreading across the country. In most cases there are nonviolent demonstrations to bring about awareness. However, our society's ability to learn seems very slow in relation to privilege and racism. Groups who felt they were being disenfranchised and losing power as white citizens have taken a more violent approach to having their voices heard. This occurred as part of a false narrative on January 6, 2021.

I want to focus this book on those who did not conduct a terrorist raid on the US Capitol. I want to focus on what isn't working for the average person and the racism that continues silently and often unconsciously within our institutions. I want to explore racism as a continuation of Constitutional failure where it needs to become visible and addressed.

The noninsurrectionist group has different layers of thought as well. Some believe their democracy is in shambles related to a Congress that is stalled out. Some are angry that the president could go unchecked as he bribed, lied, manipulated, and acted as a mob boss.

Another group is angry at the way the courts convict so many innocent people and change the rules both in the courts and in the streets because of skin color. Some people could not believe that democracy could be so cruel to immigrants when ICE agents forcibly removed children from their parents.

We rip children from parents' arms and call this our legal right because those immigrants didn't ask nicely to be citizens. ICE was given special mandates under the previous administration to deport children and families without regard for family issues and with minimal legal rationales for deportation.

One of the principles of American democracy is our stand on human rights. Our previous actions may suggest we really don't understand human rights and should not be the gatekeepers of something we fail at ourselves.

Maybe you are angry that America can leave so many people unprotected without insurance or that we have allowed millions of young people to fall into paralyzing debt from educational loans.

Constitutional failures go deeper, as we no longer have a Congress monitoring the executive branch. We have a Justice Department that is attacked by the executive branch. Maybe it is worse when the president believes the Department of Justice is his personal attorney.

We have a partisan Congress that is so divided I don't believe we can accomplish what is needed in America. The process can stall us out at every decision point. I don't see how the House of Representatives (the House) can work with the Senate unless they are dominated by the same party. Even with a simple majority, the filibuster can be used to stop all bills from moving forward, requiring a three-fifths majority to pass.

We have over a hundred congressional leaders who are in such fear of losing votes that they signed on with the State of Texas Attorney General to sue another state—a direct violation of the current Constitution (Amendment 11). Their lawsuit was rejected by the Supreme Court on arrival because of its unconstitutional stance. Who are these constitutional violators? It appears the full roster of 126 are all Republicans. How can that be? Has that party fallen into some deep abyss where their minds were drained of constitutional law? Here they are:

Alabama
Robert B. Aderholt
Mo Brooks
Bradley Byrne
Gary Palmer
Mike D. Rogers

Arizona
Andy Biggs
Debbie Lesko

Arkansas
Rick Crawford

California
Ken Calvert
Doug LaMalfa
Kevin McCarthy
Tom McClintock

Colorado
Ken Buck
Doug Lamborn

Florida
Gus Bilirakis
Mario Diaz-Balart
Neal Dunn
Matt Gaetz
Bill Posey
John Rutherford
Ross Spano
Greg Steube
Michael Waltz
Daniel Webster
Ted Yoho

Georgia
Rick Allen
Buddy Carter
Doug Collins
A. Drew Ferguson
Jody Hice
Barry Loudermilk
Austin Scott

Idaho
Russ Fulcher
Mike Simpson

Illinois
Mike Bost
Darin M. LaHood

Indiana
James Baird
Jim Banks
Trey Hollingsworth
Greg Pence
Jackie Walorski

Iowa
Steve King

Kansas
Ron Estes
Roger Marshall

Louisiana
Ralph Abraham
Clay Higgins
Mike Johnson
Steve Scalise

Maryland
Andy Harris

Michigan
Jack Bergman
Bill Huizenga
John Moolenaar
Tim Walberg

Minnesota
Tom Emmer
Jim Hagedorn
Pete Stauber

Mississippi
Michael Guest
Trent Kelly
Steven Palazzo

Missouri
Sam Graves
Vicky Hartzler
Billy Long
Blaine Luetkemeyer
Jason Smith
Ann Wagner

Montana
Greg Gianforte

Nebraska
Jeff Fortenberry
Adrian Smith

New Jersey
Jefferson Van Drew

New York
Elise Stefanik
Lee Zeldin

North Carolina
Dan Bishop
Ted Budd
Virginia Foxx
Richard Hudson
Greg Murphy
David Rouzer
Mark Walker

Ohio
Bob Gibbs
Bill Johnson
Jim Jordan
Robert E. Latta
Brad Wenstrup

Oklahoma
Kevin Hern
Markwayne Mullin

Pennsylvania
John Joyce
Fred Keller
Mike Kelly
Daniel Meuser
Scott Perry
Guy Reschenthaler
Glenn Thompson

South Carolina
Jeffrey Duncan
Ralph Norman
Tom Rice
William Timmons
Joe Wilson

Tennessee
Tim Burchett
Scott DesJarlais
Chuck Fleischmann
Mike Green
David Kustoff
John Rose

Texas
Jodey Arrington
Brian Babin
Kevin Brady
Michael C. Burgess
Michael Cloud
K. Michael Conaway
Dan Crenshaw
Bill Flores
Louie Gohmert
Lance Gooden
Kenny Marchant
Randy Weber
Roger Williams
Ron Wright

Virginia
Ben Cline
Morgan Griffith
Robert J. Wittman

Washington
Cathy McMorris Rodgers
Dan Newhouse

West Virginia
Carol Miller
Alex Mooney

Wisconsin
Tom Tiffany

I put their names in here because they are active Congressional members of the House. They have yet to face any consequences for violating the Constitution and their oath of office.

President Trump asked Russia and Ukraine to help him find information on those he was running against in the 2016 election and presented a quid pro quo request to the president of the Ukraine to get additional dirt on his opponent's son. This is not in dispute, but it seems there is no consequence to violating Article II, Section 4, which states that the president "shall be removed from office and impeached for, and conviction of treason, **bribery**, and other high crimes and misdemeanors." This occurs because the evidence is used in the House to impeach an elected official, while the Senate has the right to decide if they will convict the person. In all four impeachment cases in our US history, the Senate has never convicted the person

In recent days immediate proof of the Russians being actively involved in supporting the Trump election has come to light. How did President Trump miss being punished post-impeachment for such actions? He was impeached by the House twice but acquitted both times by the Senate. Maybe impeachment is not used correctly, or has flaws needing correcting?

Will there be consequences in the future? Time will tell, but I don't believe impeachment is a remedy that can work in today's Congress. We have recent examples of its complete failure to hold the executive accountable for violating their oath of office. I don't believe in constitutional and oath violations without a person having a consequence. There is something wrong when such behavior is acceptable in a democratic country.

Another serious problem is how we are taxed. How can the richest companies in America pay zero percent in federal taxes and then get millions in tax rebates on top of their earnings? Amazon in 2018 made $10.8 billion and paid no taxes, with a $128 million rebate. General Motors and Netflix paid no federal taxes. President Trump paid less than $1,000 a few years ago in federal taxes, as have many millionaires under current tax laws. The New York Times once had a full-page ad where billionaires all said they need to be taxed.

We have billionaires and special interest groups with more power than American citizens regarding Congress's actions or US policy. Lobbyists push agendas that may go against what people want, and congressional leaders follow the lobbyists' agenda.

One classic example is how the National Rifle Association (NRA) can keep Congress from writing a law that mandates background checks on all gun sales. Many states allow no background checks for personal sales or gun show sales and there is no congressional energy to overcome the NRA's push to keep it this way.

We allow dark money to be pushed into our election system, so we don't know who is paying for an election. Jane Mayer wrote a book called *Dark Money: The Hidden History of the Billionaires behind the Rise of the Radical Right* (2017). She describes her findings after hundreds of interviews exposing the way billionaires are infiltrating the conservative movement to place specific people in power. This points our country and political decisions in a specific direction—the direction of the money. Texas, as recently as May, 2021, now allows any person the age of 21 to purchase a gun without any background check. Is this how we want our country, campaigns, laws, and elections to function?

Conservative money was able to bring in "Citizens United" to allow nonprofit organizations and unions to conduct political activities and to end funding limits on campaigns as well. One outcome of this ruling is allowing corporations to be equal to individuals. I wonder if a corporation can be executed for a crime like a person in the state of Texas?

The Supreme Court has had several split decisions in favor of allowing unlimited funding to political campaigns. Part of the Supreme Court sees this as a First Amendment issue. The other half does not. It brings up two serious concerns. The first is our acceptance of close or split Supreme Court decisions as law even though there is an obvious difference in how that law is being interpreted. The second is how the Supreme Court has aligned with the concept of dark money that can sway American values and our constitutional impact on US policies. Here is a document worth reading regarding the impact the Supreme Court has had on allowing dark money into our campaigns: http://www.demos.org/sites/default/files/publications/Money%20in%20Politics%20FAQ_0.pdf (This is a public service document).

The Supreme Court cases that over time allowed dark money into the campaign process are seen in Table 1.

Table 1. Cases in which the Supreme Court allowed dark money to enter the campaign process

Year	Case	Limits on decision	Justice vote
1976	Buckley v. Valeo	Overall campaign spending, candidate personal spending, and independent expenditures can't be capped.	5 to 3
2007	Wisconsin Right to Life v. FEC	The government can't halt outside group political advertising in the period before an election.	5 to 4
2008	FEC v. Davis	The government can't let opponents of self-financed candidates exceed the usual contribution limits.	5 to 4
2010	Citizens United v. FEC	No limits on the amount of outside spending are permissible, and corporations can spend directly on campaigns.	5 to 4
2011	Arizona Free Enterprise Club's Freedom PAC v. Bennet	Public financing systems can't use escalating matching funds.	5 to 4
2014	McCutcheon v. FEC	A donor's overall spending on federal campaigns can't be capped.	5 to 4

This table shows how the court has continued to have decisions that allow for extravagant political donations and a continuation of the court's split votes. The continued acceptance of dark money in a democracy pushes against the meaning of "by and for the people."

How are such abuses possible in a democracy with our Constitution? I continue to be confused regarding how people can take an oath to uphold the Constitution and then violate that oath with no consequences. Where is our moral compass related to being an American citizen? I want to pound control alt delete on my computer as a way to have a complete reboot!

I understand that we have had some of these issues for as long as we have attempted to care about democracy. It is time to take a quick tour of our past because all this crazy behavior did not occur only in recent years.

CHAPTER 2

Historical Democracy: Actions and Failures in the United States

American democracy comes from three primary documents and a group of essays or papers:

1) The Articles of Confederation (1777),
2) The Constitution (1787–1789),
3) The Amendments to the Constitution, (1791–1992), and
4) The Federalist (Federalist Papers, 1777–1787).

We began this experiment with the Confederation Articles that were finally ratified by thirteen states in 1777. The eighty-seven Federalist (Papers) essays were used from 1777 to 1787 to help the founders clarify what they believed needed correcting. These documents and some revolutionary actions brought in a revised and new US Constitution that began to be ratified in 1787 and was finalized in 1789 by all the States.

Shays' Rebellion of 1786 shined a beacon of light on the Articles of the Confederation's weaknesses, which did not include a section discussing taxation of our citizens.

Shay had a militia of over one thousand armed, rebellious farmers who did not believe Massachusetts's taxation process was appropriate. After serving in the Revolutionary War with minimal or no pay, they returned to their farms and were told to pay back taxes, but they did not have the funds.

Shay formed a military rebellion that proved unsuccessful in the end. Shay's men planned to attack the Springfield Arsenal and take the weapons they might need. However, four thousand US troops stopped the rebellion with only three dead and twenty wounded. The courts, popular sentiment, and a new governor led to a pardon for Shay and those who went with him. He died with a strong following in 1825 in Sparta, New York, but he changed American history, as his rebellion showed a need for a revised Constitution.

The 1787 updated Constitution contains seven articles with many sections under each article, and includes twenty-seven amendments, beginning in 1791. You can read what is in the Constitution and its amendments in Appendices I and II.

The big question we need to grapple with is, "What should be in the Constitution today?" How is it possible to believe in the power and value of the past democratic process after what has been seen in our past as well as in recent events? What do you think needs to change regarding this document?

Since our desire to be a democratic nation under the Articles of Confederation in 1777, we have taken land and slaughtered the Native Americans to support westward expansion. We didn't revise this history; we just don't like to acknowledge it.

We move forward one hundred years with a new Constitution as Americans continue to battle and kill the indigenous peoples of the United States to take their land and drive out the "savage" by forcing their young people into religious schools. I will acknowledge the move west did kill many settlers and soldiers. Still, the loss of human life was much greater for the American Indian tribes.

The climax between the native people and the United States came in 1812 after Indian tribes joined the British-Ireland opposition but were defeated by the United States military. This win strengthened a nationalism mentality.

The Indian Removal Act of 1830 authorized the movement of Indian tribes to designated reservations. The Indian Peoples were pushed and slaughtered on this journey as well. This era was considered genocide and called the Trail of Tears. It discriminated against and exterminated a specific ethnic group in huge numbers, which is the definition of genocide. The government's relationship with the native population was a painful failure of early democracy in America.

Another painful failure occurred after the Civil War. The United States did not help African Americans after the US Civil War ended in 1867. We had a revised Constitution that proclaimed all men were created equal. Still, at the same time, we claimed slavery was our right and a part of our culture up to the end of the Civil War. The postwar political battles created other racist issues, and the goal was to keep African Americans from sitting, educating, eating, and traveling equally with white people.

More recently we are finally hearing what happened in 1921 in Tulsa, OK. There was a very progressive community of African Americans who were building a prosperous life for the segregated town of Tulsa. However, this community was crushed, burned, bombed, and finally destroyed. No one was held accountable. No one wanted this in the history books. *Black Wall Street* was destroyed because it was becoming equal in a white privileged America. This event was so hidden, I didn't even know it occurred until I was getting ready to send this book to print.

Even today, American institutions continue to struggle with bias, discrimination, and unequal democracy for people of color. We are now facing a continuation of implicit biases within law enforcement, housing, and other segments of our society. There is a belief that some Americans will lose something if they are placed as equals with minority groups. We really have a long way to go in practical terms, not just in how we understand democracy.

When America needed these minority groups, we put them into a quiet and hidden area to use their talents but did not let them be equal. Several minority groups were of extreme value in American history and included the Tuskegee Airmen, Navajo code talkers, Jewish researchers and engineers, the thirty-three thousand Japanese working as translators, and the famous 442nd from Hawaii, which was an all-Japanese regiment fighting for the United States during World War II.

American society didn't let women have equal rights with their male partners for various reasons throughout most of history. Women were not allowed to have their own money, obtain credit, own property, or have voting rights. This was a constant struggle into the 20th century. Congress has an equal pay bill for women and men that seems to be stuck as I am writing this. I wonder what the real reason is for such resistance to equality for women?

It seems we have always struggled to have a democracy for all. American democracy stewards have done all these things to keep the power and decision making in the hands of only a few. Our past and current experiences are a democratic tragedy, and it has occurred under our current US Constitution and amendments.

CHAPTER 3

Recent Democracy Failures

When we hold an election, it becomes a comedy show of truth, lies, propaganda, foreign influences, and dark money. You can win by three million votes and lose an election because we hold a strange belief—that your vote will count to elect the president. However, your vote only counts for your state to know which way its Electoral College delegates will be voting. That is written into the Constitution, but is this what we want? Your vote counts, but not in the way you think. The majority votes of a state push that state to use its Electoral College delegates to send an overall state vote to the legislature, except for two states who can split electoral votes. When the candidate receives 270 electoral votes, they become the president elect. This is true even if the popular vote went for the other candidate, as was seen in Hillary Clinton versus Donald Trump in 2016.

In 2020 we heard representatives, senators, and the president saying that Congress could overturn all the Electoral College votes to choose the president themselves. That was in blatant contradiction to the Constitution. Was anyone charged for violating this Constitutional Article? In 2020, some challenges to the final votes were stopped by state legislatures and the Supreme Court, who made final rulings to reject all the challenges as being baseless. President Trump's legal team sent approximately sixty challenges to the courts, which found all challenges illegal or without merit. So, how were Trump's attorneys ever allowed to make such claims without consequences in the first place? Can we pound the judicial system with a barrage of filings and not have to pay a price if they are illegal, unconstitutional, or without any merit?

Actions taken during the 2020 elections show us the fallacy of trusting our leaders to keep a moral focus and follow the Constitution. In the end, you might believe the Constitution held. I believe it is holding on by a thread. There is no apparent consequence for trying to violate the Constitution or for making false claims based on conspiracy theories that impact American institutions and the concept of truth.

The Trump presidency and the 2020 election have been the greatest examples of how democracy is ruptured, out of date, and a lie to most Americans. How are we as a nation to respond to one of the three government branches not following the rules or traditions of our society? What if one branch ignores its oath to the Constitution? What if one branch uses power in a way never used before? Will the Constitution continue to hold up? I don't believe it can.

Look at these statements we often think of as true:

- There is a balance of power—not true!
- The Supreme Court is nonpartisan—not true!
- We take care of Americans who are in need—sometimes.
- Congress is the voice of the people—not true!
- Capitalism works for all Americans—not true!
- The legal system provides justice for all—not true!
- Everyone pays their fair share in taxes—not true!
- No one is above the law—not true!
- We are a moral democracy in the world—sometimes.
- All persons have a right to protection under the law—not true!

Part of our democracy and rulings rests with the Supreme Court, which has lifelong members who are theoretically nonpartisan. Their rulings were meant to address interpretations of actions based on the Constitution of the United States. The general population does not have a clear understanding of how Supreme Court decisions impact their lives.

Sometimes a court decision has an impact not immediately seen but that can have tremendous effects in the future.

Here is a website that has many landmark decisions made by the Supreme Court over the years that can be seen as negatively impacting all of us: https://www.gopopro.com/landmark-court-cases-1/2017/2/15/citizens-united-v-federal-election-commission-fec. (It is worth a look.)

One powerful example of what the Supreme Court is supposed to do is protect the right of all people to a life of liberty and protection under the Fourteenth Amendment. This expectation of being protected may not always come true.

Ms. Gonzales had a permanent protection order against her former husband. Still, her husband had a right to a specified visitation under significant restrictions when visiting his three daughters. In 1999, the police were notified the husband had violated the visitation and did not bring his three daughters back to the house when they were to be returned. The police were notified a second time that the husband had taken the girls to another location, which also violated the order. Ms. Gonzales warned the police about her husband's dangerous past behaviors and showed the police the order.

Early the next morning, the husband drove up to the police department and started a gunfight, where he was killed. Ms. Gonzales's three daughters were found shot to death in the back seat, which he had done the previous evening. No one knows his intention for coming to the police except that he had killed his children and may have wanted to be killed himself.

Ms. Gonzales claimed her liberty was violated, which was heard by the Tenth Circuit Court of Colorado. The motion was classified as a legal opinion regarding a federally protected property interest mandate under the Constitution. Ms. Gonzales stated there was no enforcement of the restraining order, alleging "an official policy or custom of failing to respond properly to complaints of restraining order violations."

A motion to dismiss the case was granted, and Ms. Gonzales appealed to the Denver, Colorado, Tenth Circuit Court of Appeals. A panel of that court rejected Gonzales's substantive due process claim but found in her favor a procedural due process claim. The Supreme Court heard the case in 2009 and sided with the Tenth Circuit Court of Colorado and against Ms. Gonzales, where the court also affirmed that the three individual officers had qualified immunity and could not be sued for not responding to Ms. Gonzales's restraining order violation against her husband.

Ms. Gonzales's case suggests various forms of immunity for the officers of the law. This leaves a big hole in the Fourteenth Amendment, where we might believe we have a right to be protected, which actually may not be true. Some have seen this as a right to be heard by law enforcement, but there is no requirement that they must respond to your needs.

It is a painful read: Castle Rock v. Gonzales (Supreme Court | US Law | LII / Legal Information Institute [cornell.edu]). This case is partially the reason we see so many officers not charged with crimes when they violate a person's rights during an arrest.

There are many issues currently being raised by citizens and police departments regarding what the relationship of law enforcement and the community should be. But, keep in mind that changing a Supreme Court decision will require a revision in the Constitution by an amendment, which is a significant challenge.

If we look at the narrative being espoused by QAnon, we see a huge movement that is antigovernment and full of conspiracy theories and false beliefs regarding child sacrifices, abuse, and bloodletting. The QAnon movement appears to be opposed to our current democracy for a host of reasons that go far beyond a failure by democracy to protect its citizens. They continue to build a following, as they spread lies that have been followed up by killings, insurrections, and false expectations of a Trump Savior. On June 3, 2020, a CNN report discusses what happens when QAnon believers are elected into politics. Mark Finchen is a State Representative for Arizona, and offers support for a deep state conspiracy about the abuse of children. In the 2022 election campaigns, you will find nineteen congressional races. Of the nineteen Republican candidates, you will find eighteen Republicans supporting QAnon beliefs.

What is the outcome of 20 million QAnon followers and others joining an antigovernment movement for their own reasons that are embedded in terrorist propaganda? There are many reasons why other groups might want to join an antigovernment movement, but QAnon should be labeled a terrorist group trying to bring down the institution and put a dictator in place that agrees with them. Will we be able to reboot, have more revolts, or will we plug along as we always have, thinking we are too strong for anything to really happen?

Maybe the Constitution is not what we think it is. I mentioned this earlier, but on March 29, 2021, an article by Jill Lepore appeared in The New Yorker that will shake you to your core: https://www.newyorker.com/magazine/2021/03/29/when-constitutions-took-over-the-world?

There are many powerful issues in this report, but my current concerns are related to the discussion of Kurt Gödel, the greatest logician since Aristotle. In 1947, Gödel, Einstein, and Morgenstern were working toward Gödel becoming a citizen, as his colleagues had done. Gödel was compulsive and believed he would be questioned vigorously regarding the Constitution, even though Einstein and Morgenstern said this would not happen. By the time he came for his citizenship hearing, he had discovered a major flaw in the Constitution that might not prevent the United States from falling into autocratic dictatorship. The concept has been widely studied and was give the name Gödel's Loophole.

Article V is where the Constitution describes how an amendment can be changed, and Gödel discovered there was no safeguard in that article. Nothing was preventing Article V from being changed and allowing a single person to make future amendments using current Article V guidelines. We could have thirty-eight states change Article V to include a president or a QAnon dictator making future amendments independently. If that occurred, Article V would allow for a dictator to control the Constitution.

Dennis Rasmussen argues in *Fears of a Setting Sun: The Disillusionment of America's Founders* (2021) that many of the founders had serious doubts about this new government and its success. This may be why the phrase "now see if you can keep it" is associated with the founders' guidance to those in the future.

It seems we have experienced and continue to experience the risk of a potential collapse that is still pending. Will America even want to continue as a democracy into the future? It is time for citizens to begin the discussion on what should be in the Constitution. If not now—when? If not you—who?

Let me repeat what Jefferson said in 1816 to Samuel Kercheval of Virginia, "I am not an advocate for frequent changes in laws and constitutions, but laws and institutions must go hand in hand with the progress of the human mind. As that becomes more developed, more enlightened, as new discoveries are made, new truths discovered and manners and opinions change, with the change of circumstances, institutions must advance also to keep pace with the times. We might as well require a man to wear still the coat which fitted him when a boy, as civilized society to remain ever under the regimen of their barbarous ancestors."

CHAPTER 4

Congress in Reboot

Congress has two parts: the House of Representatives and the Senate. Article I of the Constitution is dedicated to these two chambers. It was previously called the United States Assembly under the Confederation Articles and was a single chamber. There was no division of responsibilities as there is now. Under the 1787 revised Constitution, a division of power and representation of states by population was given to the House. Currently the House has 435 voting members and six nonvoting members who serve four-year terms. Nonvoting members come from the District of Columbia and the five populated territories, which are Puerto Rico, Guam, American Samoa, the US Virgin Islands, and the Northern Mariana Islands. Have you ever heard the phrase, "No taxation without representation?" Well, that is not true. We do tax these territories and do not allow them to have a voting representative.

It has been suggested that the Cherokee Nation and Choctaw Nation each have a representative. Still, they have never been seated, and we don't seem to discuss this. The Choctaw Nation has been given a right to have a House member based on their treaty, but a representative has never been allowed. Just keep quiet and no one will know that we don't care about our integrity with the Choctaw.

The Senate was meant to give each state an equal voice by having two senators each, totaling one hundred members. There are no nonvoting members, and the vice president can only vote as a tiebreaker.

Senators serve for six-year terms and have different responsibilities from the House. Both can sponsor bills that must be approved by the other chamber with or without amendments.

It is interesting to note how both groups have controlled who they are and who they represent. How is this equal among all US citizens? Is their structure the way it should be today? Imagine if the House had representatives based on the total taxes paid to the federal government versus the state's population. What if the Senate mandated a Republican and a Democrat for each state? What are some other possible changes?

The next section is where you and I submit our ideas to text. My ideas are being placed in the book, but you will need to send your ideas to the blog once you think about the needed changes. Each new idea also needs a rationale for the idea. This gives the reader more context for what is being suggested. I will include my first thoughts on each of the topics, starting with my thoughts on Congress reform.

Ctrl Alt Delete

1. House members need to have term limits for continuing their role to a maximum of twelve years (three terms).

   This allows for new blood, new ideas, and reducing the belief that the members work for themselves or special interests.

2. The Senate will be limited to a total of twelve years (two terms).

   This allows for new blood, new ideas, and reduced belief that members work for themselves or special interests.

3. Eliminate the majority leader's power by having a six-person panel, with the majority leader being the seventh nonvoting member of this six-person leadership team. The leadership team is comprised of three members from each party without any two members from the same state. This is true for the House and Senate. The majority leader only votes when there is a tie in the leader team. The

leader team makes all decisions currently being conducted by the majority leader.

This prevents too much power being given to the majority leader regardless of who is in power.

4. All compensation (salary and benefits to include all insurances) for the House will be set by the Senate and vice-versa. Compensation for the executive and Supreme Court will be set by the Senate. All compensation for federal court justices will be set by the House.

   All compensation is set for a given term in the House and Senate, with additional terms having a 5 percent increase adjustment for the additional term. All compensation ends for the House and Senate members twelve months after leaving office.

This is a way to give fair compensation for government officials. These changes will control the never ending payments being made to Congress members once leaving office. It also controls the two groups giving themselves a raise.

5. No bill can be held up by the House or by the Senate when it has been approved by its originating chamber (either the House or the Senate) if it passed that chamber by a six-tenths majority.

   One exception for this rule is when the reviewing group (the nonoriginating House or Senate) makes an amendment to the bill by a majority of the reviewing chamber's leadership team. The amendment is either approved or rejected by a majority of the leadership team of the originating chamber. The bill will move forward, be revised, or fail.

This would promote bills being moved or rejected by more than the majority of the House or the Senate, or preventing power blocks by either the majority or the majority leader.

6. Impeachments of any person in any role of the three branches of the government can be brought to a hearing by the House. Three members of the Supreme Court are chosen by the Senate's leader team to hear the evidence with "a preponderance of the evidence" being the rule of law for the justices to make a decision of guilt.

    The Senate will provide the punishment that can balance the issues of guilt but cannot determine there is no consequence if the Justices have found the person guilty..

    The minimum punishment is removal from all subcommittees, a $100,000 fine, and no executive orders. The maximum penalty is expulsion from all federal positions for life and a $100,000 fine.

This is a way to break the politics that cannot determine impeachment guilt, and keeps the House and Senate engaged in impeachments when needed.

7. There can be a filibuster by any member of the House or Senate. Still, the consequence of holding

a filibuster is for the member initiating the filibuster being required to leave his or her position within thirty days of holding that filibuster.

This is used to show a consequence of holding Congress at bay. If it is worth it, then do it with a consequence.

8. If the House or the Senate or either leadership team makes a procedural rule that may or may not have a partisan impact, the rule must be abided by for a minimum of four years. This can be overruled by a six-tenths majority of either the House or Senate, who have to abide by that rule.

This is to prevent petty rules (e.g., not being able to confirm a Supreme Court justice in the last year of a presidency that is partisan in nature and then not required to be followed in the future by another group rising to power).

9. Lobbyists are not allowed to have private meetings with any congressional member. Any lobbyist meeting must be accompanied by at least one of the opposition leader team members and a written transcript of that meeting must be published.

This is meant to reduce the lobbyists' power and to make these meetings more open.

10. No congressional member can use more than $20 million to campaign for a Senate or House position. Whatever dollars are used in a campaign, the funding group must provide equal money to support a nonprofit public program for disaster relief, homeless/food supplement care, or climate control programs.

   This would manage the excessive money being pushed into campaigns and would control dark money.

11. No public media advertising can start until three months prior to the election. This does not limit in-person speeches or television debates.

    This is meant to control the election media marketing that is overwhelming to the public and much too expensive with no benefit to public interest.

What are your ideas for changing Congress?

NOTES:

CHAPTER 5

Executive Reboot

Article II of the Constitution involves the executive branch. Many things were thought to be true regarding this office until it was stress-tested by the Trump presidency. There was a belief in place that the president could not become autocratic or take on some other role that would negatively impact democracy.

The checks-and-balances strategies do not seem to work as the founders might have intended. A president can currently attack First Amendment rights of free speech, the press, and the right of peaceful assembly; push propaganda messaging to overturn elections; and feed false information that allows for a false reality for their followers.

These actions were recently practiced by former president Donald Trump, who subsequently suffered no consequences as a result. He did many things to violate his oath, and he was twice impeached by the House, something that has never happened to any prior president. However, the Senate declined to find cause or consequences for the dangerous actions of President Trump.

Historically, impeachment is highly partisan and basically an empty threat. Taking an oath to uphold the Constitution holds no more water than a food strainer. We have seen this recently by congressional members and the president. This needs to change. We can thank the Trump presidency for showing America where democracy is not working.

It makes me concerned about the Electoral College being the final vote for putting a president into office. I worry about how it can be challenged by various persons prior to the ballots making it to Congress. We have recently experienced many risks regarding this process. You might believe democracy worked and held up under recent strains of political attack. However, it might not have held except for a few resilient individuals. It is not strong enough to be a true barrier against such constitutional attacks. This means we need to do something, and we need to do it sooner rather than later.

Recent Department of Justice statements by Attorney General William Barr suggested the president cannot be charged with a crime while in office. The Mueller report says the president cannot be charged with civil offenses while in office. Both Barr's and Mueller's statements may seem new since it has always been stated that no one is above the law.

Impeachment is limited in scope and may not cover a host of criminal offenses that could arise from a president. Our history of four impeachments suggests this is not a safeguard for the executive conducting some impeachable offense. Does our current system put the president above the law? I believe it does, and this is not acceptable. Here are my thoughts on the subject:

Ctrl Alt Delete

1. The executive can only run for a single six-year term.

   This will prevent the current president from using US resources and time to run for a second term. This is a serious waste of resources.

2. The executive compensation (all benefits, salaries, insurances) will end twelve months after leaving office. Security will continue for a total of six years after leaving office.

   This is used to control costs, prevent payments with no end, and allow the past president to be part of the regular population.

3. Presidential pardons seem to be a gift for loyal friends. This should not be provided to any

personal acquaintance, coworker, or a known friend of the president.

When it is used, the president must contribute $50,000 of his or her salary to the correctional reform projects for each pardon. The $50,000 payments will end once the president has given one year's salary to the pardon process. There are no additional fees for additional pardons once a year's salary has been spent. Pardons cannot be used as a quid pro quo action.

This is used to balance good reasoning, value, and cost to the pardon process and eliminate its use as a quid pro quo action.

4. All three branches of the government will require that any person running for office must provide up to ten years' worth of tax returns. These tax returns must be released to the public as a part of the application process.

This will provide a higher ethical standard to the application process for the three branches of government.

What do you believe needs a control alt delete in the executive branch?

NOTES:

CHAPTER 6

Supreme Court and Federal Courts in Reboot

Supreme Court justices were meant to be nonpartisan, but this has not been the case based on their voting records being more liberal, moderate, or conservative. This positioning puts them onto a partisan platform, and it has been very controversial over the years. Federal courts may have a similar partisan issue, as does the Supreme Court because they are all picked by the current president and then confirmed by the Senate.

Article III of the Constitution discusses the rules for the judicial branch of the federal government. This includes the Supreme Court as well as lower courts created by Congress. It provides a host of areas for which all the federal courts are responsible.

The Supreme Court is a final reviewer of disputes over the meaning of laws and how the law aligns with the Constitution. This is an asset to a fluid democracy with cultural changes over time.

However, some cases can push the rational-thinking boundaries of our society. The Castle Rock versus Gonzales and Citizens United cases presented in this book suggest there are serious issues related to the Supreme Court's decisions. These cases seem to violate all normal thinking regarding how we want laws for the people's best interests.

Currently the courts do not address impeachment, but rather this is left to Congress to address. This may or may not be a valuable position as we look at the weak and ineffective impeachment process.

The previous impeachment cases in our history seem to be fluid and political. Maybe the courts need to be more involved to reduce the partisan nature of the impeachment process as discussed earlier.

Justices and judges are lifelong appointees, and this seems to raise other issues. Also, there is no financial assessment or past tax assessment for justices as there is for judges.

Here are my thoughts on what might be good changes to this group:

Ctrl Alt Delete

1. All Supreme Court justices can hold office for a maximum of eighteen years, not for life.

This is to prevent the idea that such positions are overly powerful by their permanency.

2. Pay is set by the Senate, and increases can only be made at 5 percent every five years. All salaries and benefits end twelve months after leaving office for any reason. Security is provided for twelve months after leaving office.

   This is used to control the endless cost of such positions but offer some security after leaving office.

3. Federal judges can be replaced by the next elected president after five years of service and cannot be in an equivalent position for more than eighteen years total.

   They could move from one type of court to another type of court within the federal system but cannot be in any federal court position for more than twenty-five years total. All salaries and benefits end twelve months after leaving office.

   This would be a way to keep some turnover for federal judges, but not a constant turnover. Also, presidents will be unable to replace anyone who does not have a minimum of five years of service to prevent an excessive expulsion of judges.

4. The number of Supreme Court justices would be set at nine, and they would have to be replaced within sixty days of a justice vacancy.

   This would only be true if there were term limits in

place. It would also prevent delays in putting someone onto the Supreme Court, regardless of who is president.

5. All Supreme Court opinions that become law cannot arise from an equal split with the chief justice making a final vote. Such votes should be redirected by the chief justice to where the first court ruled using the appeals court's information and the Supreme Court's comments to make another ruling. The chief justice will rule if there is a justice who abstains for ethical reasons.

Split votes do not appear to have a singular legal thread of thinking. That leaves people to wonder how the ruling can be divided if the justices are nonbiased and using the rule of law to guide them. There must also be an ethical reason for a justice to abstain.

6. Federal courts will only have three-judge panels, where they must have a majority ruling for convictions. Jury trials are eliminated. There is now a science of juror assessments, and jury lawyers are experts in manipulating thinking to end with a verdict not related to the facts. Grand Jury evidence reviews will still be used to see if there is evidence to go to trial.

Jury trials by individuals are now a science of who can manipulate jurors' choices and how they think. Normal public citizens are not known for objectivity; most are not data driven or rational by nature. People cannot control their implicit bias imprinting. Most normal people do not understand the law. Regular people could never explain the difference between "the preponderance of the evidence" and "beyond a reasonable doubt."

7. We need to rethink the language of guilty "beyond a reasonable doubt." Any alternative narrative of the crime can create a reasonable doubt. Widely-known research shows that humans confuse, distort, or misread what they believe they have seen, and proficient attorneys can use such research to show reasonable doubt.

The idea of reasonable doubt is a confusing standard of guilt that is not based on facts.

What are your ideas for the Supreme Court and federal court system?

NOTES:

CHAPTER 7

State Criminal System in Reboot

The state criminal justice system has received significant attention for many reasons in the past few years. This movement may be a refinement movement versus a control alt delete process. Here are just a few of the issues currently in place.

Drug reforms on incarceration for minor use or minimal possession were enacted on November 3, 2020. The people voted for such reforms in Arizona, Montana, New Jersey, and South Dakota. Oregon moved such offenses to be low-level civil cases that are resolved by fines. Colorado, Oklahoma, and other states have moved drug possession charges to be classified as misdemeanor offenses. Michigan is joining five other states to expunge past records, so their citizens can have all rights, including voting rights, restored. Some expungements will be automatic, but others need to be requested.

California, under Governor Newsom, has signed ten different bills addressing various aspects of criminal reform. It is easy to see a movement to address this part of our democracy. Unfortunately, states have the right to create their own laws, and some states move in a different direction.

Florida has unveiled new legislation to criminalize as a felony the act of blocking a road. Florida also increased its executions before there could be a new administration that might eliminate capital punishment.

Some states increase punishments as other states reduce them. Currently, our Constitution supports such individuality of states. Maybe states need to be reexamined as to what they have control over and how we might be more uniform in our justice systems.

Why do we say a spouse cannot be asked to give evidence against his or her partner? Why can't we use evidence—regardless of where it comes from—if it hasn't been fabricated or coerced? Why can't we use the results of a lie-detector test for some issues? Why do we use plaintiff testimony when we manipulate the conversation or set up a fatigue syndrome that can confuse any mind? This is actually a form of military interrogation and has not been seen as getting to the factual issues.

What does it mean to have a "jury of one's peers"? How did we get so many innocent people convicted and jailed with eyewitness testimony? Who needs protection more—society or the person or entity that has been charged? All these issues need to be looked at again.

Another issue is how the courts differentiate between a person being found guilty for a civil offense versus being found guilty for a criminal offense. I believe the criminal system needs a *reboot*.

As a reminder, the criminal system says a person can be found guilty using the definition of guilt as "beyond a reasonable doubt."

A civil guilty outcome is based on "a preponderance of the evidence." Does anyone believe a good attorney cannot find a reasonable doubt on any prosecution case? Do you remember the saying, "if it does not fit, you must acquit"? This idea pushed a reasonable doubt. We now live in a post-truth world, and it is run on various versions of doubt, even in the face of facts. We must look at this more closely for a fair trial system to work at all. If the George Floyd murder trial did not have a video but only the testimony of the witnesses present, is it possible the jury would have found reasonable doubt? Was the video the part that prevented reasonable doubt? I believe the answer is YES!

Ctrl Alt Delete

1. Criminal and civil trials will only use the definition of "a preponderance of the evidence" and eliminate the definition "beyond a reasonable doubt" as defining a person's guilt or innocence.

   This would avoid a definition that cannot hold up in our current post-truth world.

2. We do not have a trial by our peers. We currently have a right to a jury trial, but this needs to be revised for criminal cases. Criminal trials should have a three-judge panel or some other legal assessment forum that avoids the general public.

   This change is needed because people are not rational but make decisions based on bias, values, personal culture, and emotional impact and are rarely based on facts. We now have a host of people who believe in the idea of alternative facts, or the idea that my facts differ from your facts.

3. There is a need for all municipalities and police responses to have a different view of their roles. The engagement of social workers, mental health workers, counselors, arbitrators, and health care professionals should attend 911 calls in conjunction with police to provide the correct response for criminal or confusing non-violent behaviors.

   This would look like the fire department that attends all

911 medical calls and would eliminate police officers being asked to deal with issues beyond their expertise.

4. House arrest should be used in much greater numbers, using higher levels of technology to offset incarcerations.

   This would change our way of thinking regarding incarceration and our prison system.

5. Crimes committed with a gun or any lethal device should have a higher consequence. Such crimes should be considered an extreme criminal offense requiring more controlling consequences.

   I am not sure what the consequence should be, but it needs to be strong enough to slow or stop the use of weapons during criminal activity.

What do you believe needs to be changed in the civil and criminal system today?

NOTES:

CHAPTER 8

First Amendment in Reboot

(Specific to Free Speech & Media, and Freedom of Religion)

Freedom of speech is part of the First Amendment. There has historically been a limit to speech being completely unlimited in scope. If what you say creates a clear and present danger, even if your speech does not result in definite harm, the First Amendment was not intended to protect you. However, this has become very confusing over the years.

More recently, the Supreme Court has called the few exceptions to the First Amendment "well-defined and narrowly limited." In most recent cases, we see a Court that allows for most any language to be used under the First Amendment. In the 2017 Supreme Court opinion on a trademark name that is offensive to many, (Matal v. Tam), stated the government may not prohibit expression merely because it is offensive. However in 1969 (Brandenburg v. Ohio), the Court stated one could not advocate for a crime if it "directed to inciting or producing immanent lawless actions" or its advocacy is likely to incite or produce such action. This seems to still be the opinion of the Supreme Court as again clarified in Schenck v. United States (1919), where Justice Oliver Wendell Holmes Jr. observed: "The question in every case is whether the words used are used in such circumstances and are of such a nature as to create a clear and present danger that they will bring about the substantive evils that Congress has a right to prevent." Holmes again referred to the long-standing unacceptable speech when a person who falsely shouts "Fire!" in a crowded theatre and causes a panic.

In 1940 our controls were more rigorous and Title 1 of the Smith Act found it to be a crime if someone were to advocate for the overthrow of the government. The Court has flopped repeatedly on obscenity, defamation, fraud, and any type of anti-government rhetoric, but now sees this as free speech.

What if your speech is false and inflammatory? Today this is protected as your right to an opinion. If you use hate or false statements about a public figure, it usually cannot be stopped unless you meet the proof of intentional malice, which is very difficult to prove. Our free speech confusion is a result of the Supreme Court, state laws, and Congress constantly jumping in different directions on the issue. One day there is a Sedition Act, and then it is voided. Later it is brought back and then it is voided again.

We are systemically confused as it took until 1939 before the Bill of Rights was accepted by Georgia, Massachusetts, and Connecticut. We have such diverse thinking by the states, and if combined with different opinions by the federal regulators or the Supreme Court, we end up in a democracy of free speech confusion. What are the current Constitutional interpretations of the Articles and Amendments versus how they were written? A review of the First Amendment timeline should make you wonder. (https://www.mtsu.edu/first-amendment/page/first-amendment-timeline)

I believe it is time to reboot this area of our Constitution, but it will be very difficult. We might have to get real creative to see how it can be made clearer for us—the people.

Another topic under the First Amendment is the idea of separation between church and state. It is very difficult to accomplish this separation in a society that is so active in both. Churches use state resources or have access to them for a fee. Again, we see variations by state. These organizations are a part of the entire system and cannot be excluded because of what they do. Do you believe churches should remain tax exempt in order to have some separation from the government? I don't believe so and the issues go even deeper.

Our country started by honoring all that we have being related to a God, and we put this on our money and government buildings. Today we might not do that, as we want to be inclusive to everyone's views.

There is a strong movement to create a separation that may not be possible.

We stop prayers in schools but have continued them in legislative settings. Greece v. Galloway, 572 U.S., 134 S. Ct. 1811 (2014), continues to keep this controversy going. The Greece v. Galloway Supreme Court case directly addressed the issue of prayer at governmental meetings for the first time since the Marsh v. Chambers, 463 U.S. 783 (1983). The Court ruled 5-4 to allow municipal or county bodies to begin meetings with prayers even if they were sectarian and espousing a certain belief. This ruling shocked those who believed there was a strong constitutional separation between church and state.

It seems the First Amendment is again caught in confusing rulings that fall into a battle between our original beliefs and our desire to appease everyone. There has also been the "Godless Invocation" phenomenon. Here is a part of one by Juan Mendez of Arizona in 2013.

> "… Most prayers in this room begin with a request to bow your heads. I would like to ask that you not bow your heads. I would like to ask that you take a moment to look around the room at all of the men and women here, in this moment, sharing together this extraordinary experience of being alive and of dedicating ourselves to working

toward improving the lives of the people in our state.

This is a room in which there are many challenging debates, many moments of tension, of ideological division, of frustration. But this is also a room where, as my Secular Humanist tradition stresses, by the very fact of being human, we have much more in common than we have differences. We share the same spectrum of potential for care, for compassion, for fear, for joy, for love..."

I don't disagree with what was said, but it is not an invocation to have a higher power to come and watch over the group. Look how fast we can get lost between the idea of a God versus no God in a country that also says, "I pledge allegiance to the flag of the United States of America, and to the Republic for which it stands, one nation, under God, indivisible, with liberty and justice for all." This was the form it took in 1954 and is used to this day.

However, Frances Bellamy's (1892) original creation was, "I pledge allegiance to my Flag and the Republic for which it stands, one nation, indivisible, with liberty and justice for all." In 1923 it was changed to say, "...the flag of the United Stats of America." It was the US fight against communism that pushed President Eisenhower to ask Congress to add, "under God." In our current day battle on this topic, I am amazed the current Pledge of Allegiance has stayed as is since 1954—Thank God.

What do you think it means to have separation between church and state? How separate is separate? If a church is on fire, should a locally paid fire department respond? What about police responding if there is a shooting? Can churches pay their pastor millions of dollars per year if they have such resources? Can we ever integrate the ideas of a Christian God, versus the God of Islam, the God of the Jews, or Jehovah? How do atheists fit into this mix?

Should any non-profit, whether religious or not, be exempt from taxes? Do nonprofits benefit from tax-funded municipal services?

Ctrl Alt Delete

1. I want a governmental agency—called the "Truth and Facts" Agency—that is nonpartisan and connected to the FBI. This group will have access to FBI data files with appropriate controls, yet with privacy maintained. They will make a ruling of what is considered truth, possible truth, or false statements. Any confirmed false statement would not be allowed to be perpetuated in any open social or public media or presented in a public

forum. If this occurs, it would be a felony or an impeachable offense.

Any media group publishing such documented falsehoods would also be open to criminal prosecution or fines. The process of assessing the factual truth of various ideas or charges would be a factual investigation as in any criminal complaint but aimed at factual findings not to be challenged in any court. Any "possible truth" must show competing arguments and facts. Any "truth" decision would be like a Supreme Court ruling and have to be published by the facts used to determine its validity.

This would control what is being perpetuated as true when there are no facts to suggest it. It prevents those who would say anything enough times in the hope that it becomes true in the minds of those hearing the message. It would be used to prevent fraud upon our society through false claims.

2. Free speech needs a much tighter and more comprehensive structure. It has flip-flopped over the years based on the sway of the Supreme Court. I believe some older rules need to be brought back: no incitement propaganda of any form, no burning of the American flag, no false attacks on any person, no hate speech, no publications from any organization considered to be an internal or

external terrorist group, and no preventing of a free press using journalistic ethical rules.

This would allow for a sane understanding of supporting ethical behavior in a civilized society regarding free speech.

3. Another section of the First Amendment says that there will be no law to control an established religion and no taxation of churches. We often think of this as separation of church and state under the Constitution but it is unclear in many ways as previously discussed.

   Religious and nonprofit organizations take advantage of public services and yet do not pay taxes. There is a rule to compensate the executives of nonprofits and churches for being paid a fair market wage for that position. Many such executives are now being taxed for excessive compensation beyond those fair market wages. I believe that is a good idea and should continue.

   The entire process is messy and needs an equitable way to exist in our society using local, state, and federal resources. Here are my thoughts on the matter:

   No churches or nonprofit organizations will have specific legislation against their organization's purpose, values, and social role unless it violates other constitutional issues, including the revised amendments. The organizations will be taxed using a societal minimum tax of 5 percent of gross revenues to pay for all organizations' and citizens' social services.

Executive and board members will also pay income taxes based on this minimum rate if compensation is at fair market value. For any wages greater than the fair market value, the recipients will be taxed as regular individuals.

This stops the impossible "separation of church and state," which does not really exist. It also gives some cost to the organizations that are not supposed to be in the job of creating profits. The gross income tax suggests a new way to tax, using a 5 percent tax on gross revenues. This eliminates strategies for reducing a taxable income.

What are your ideas for the First Amendment?

NOTES:

CHAPTER 9

Education in Reboot

We have an educational system with a long history of being more accessible than that of many other parts of the world. There is no constitutional area for this discussion, but it seems import for me to bring it up anyway. Our educational system has been associated with racial bias, economic privilege, and quid pro quo behaviors. For many years there was an affirmative action law to bring about a better racial balance, but nine states have banned affirmative action: California (1996), Washington (1998), Florida (1999), Michigan (2006), Nebraska (2008), Arizona (2010), New Hampshire (2012), Oklahoma (2012), and Idaho (2020). Texas had a ban in 1996, but it was reversed in 2003. As a result, we continue to struggle with how to make education racially equitable.

The cost of higher education has created an economic bias for being a student at the best academic organizations. We might not want to remember this, but higher education started out in America as a white, male, religious, family privileged system. Over time, there were continuous changes to address the new constitutional republic to become what the founders were hoping to create. However, even during the nineteenth century, the higher education system was still biased toward white males of privilege and money.

The middle of the nineteenth century started to see significant changes for African American women and men, as special universities were created for them. The mid-1800s saw the founding of such universities and colleges as Howard, Fisk, Xavier, Tuskegee, Hampton, Morehouse, Florida A & M, North Carolina, A & T State, Claflin, Delaware State, Morgan State, and Tougaloo College.

Most of these colleges and universities were founded near the 1865 date of the Thirteenth Amendment, which states, "Neither slavery nor involuntary servitude, except as a punishment for crime whereof the party shall have been duly convicted, shall exist within the United States, or any place subject to their jurisdiction." This supersedes Article IV, Section 2, of the Constitution.

This period also put a stamp of closure to slavery at the close of the Civil War. However, there continued to be serious disparity between males and females, and the races.

Spelman was the first African American women's college. It was founded in 1881, fifty years after

Wesleyan College (1836) was founded as the first (white) women's higher education facility. It wasn't until 1965 that an African American woman attended Wesleyan College. These dates suggest a slow progress for democratic rights in higher education for all those who were not white men of privilege.

America also has a policy regarding free education for primary and secondary education but then stops the free pass after that. Unfortunately, many costs for primary and secondary education are no longer covered by local taxes or are not funded.

This causes a host of funding strategies currently used to pay for certain programs within local schools. Some have suggested we should fund state colleges and universities, but that is still in debate.

What does our educational system need from a constitutional standpoint? Maybe the only issue is who might be able to attend for free. Maybe a free education should be offered only at our community colleges or in the first two years of a university.

The issues of segregation, racial bias, gender bias, and other concerns of higher education are starting to be addressed.

There are internal issues (e.g., tenure, publish or perish) and what constitutes scholarship for faculty. These will not be addressed here but need further discussion and debate.

Here are my thoughts on education reform:

Ctrl Alt Delete

Education should be a right for all Americans or those in America who are awaiting citizenship. This right extends through K-12 and for two years of technical education or four years at a college or university. After completing the higher education portion of one's education, the student will owe society one or more years of service in an approved social service/public health/military position or approved worksites for students to use their new skills for the greater social good.

We would need to determine what programs serve society for paying back the free technical or higher education received. A student could opt out all but one year of service by paying for his or her own education, but all US citizens who are postsecondary graduates would need to provide at least one year of societal service, even if they dropped out of high school.

This allows all students eighteen or older to provide a service to our democratic system. In years past, we used this system to build our parks and roads and provide work for young men who were not drafted into the military for service. It allows the younger generations to take on some level of support for their country in the form of service.

What are your ideas for the future of education in America?

NOTES:

CHAPTER 10

Taxation in Reboot

We must change our tax code, which was 2,600 pages in 2014 and is now 6,550 pages. The tax code is this way because of special interests being placed in the code. I want to assume we can have a simple individual tax code, a business/corporate tax code, and a nonprofit/religious tax code. This chapter will address federal taxes and leave state taxes for another time.

We could assume that all taxes are based on gross revenues. It would be up to an individual or company to figure out how to keep their costs down. I am starting with this premise: there is no deductible income. It seems like a good thing to have exemptions like supporting nonprofit organizations or giving individuals a tax credit because they are serving in the military or doing a societal service mandated by the government. Maybe we need a couple of these to stay in place. However, exemptions have been a curse and a blessing causing constant confusion. Maybe we just keep the rate reasonable and then make it progressive as the incomes go up?

Here are my thoughts on this issue:

Ctrl Alt Delete

1. Individual taxes must be based on gross revenue for any individual or married couple if filing jointly. No taxes should be required of anyone who makes less than $25,000 annually or $50,000 jointly. Table 2 shows the tax structure I propose.

   This is created to have progressive and proportional taxation at all levels and still generate solid revenue for the federal government.

Table 2. Federal Taxes on Gross Personal Income

	Income Range ($)		Tax Rate (%)
Single	25,000		0
Joint	50,000		0
Single	25,001	40,000	1
Joint	50,001	80,000	1
Single	40,001	75,000	4
Joint	80,001	150,000	4
Single	75,001	150,000	6
Joint	150,001	300,000	6
Single	150,001	300,000	9
Joint	300,001	450,000	9
Single	300,001	450,000	12
Joint	450,001	1,000,000	12
Single	450,001	1,000,000	20
Joint	1,000,001	2,000,000	20
Single	1,000,001	50M	25
Joint	2,000,001	100M	25
All Income	>100M		30

2 Corporate taxes will also be based on gross revenues, with deductions for expansion only. Expansion is calculated by increased revenues or additional full-time hires.

Executive compensation for the top three corporate executives will be taxed 40 percent of salaries and benefit compensation in a separate tax. Gross revenues will be as shown in Table 3.

Table 3. Federal Taxes on Gross Corporate Earnings

Gross Corporate Earnings ($)	Tax Rate (%)
< 1,000,000	5
1M–10M	8
>10M–100M	10
>100M–500M	12
>500M	15

This is offered because many companies don't pay taxes or pay only minimal taxes by deducting a host of losses. That should be a part of all businesses, as it is expected they make money and pay their fair share of taxes for their company's size and gross revenues. The corporate tax, whether 20 percent or 30 percent, does not work. There are too many holes in the code preventing an expected taxation process for companies.

3. Nonprofit and religious taxes should be a flat rate of 5 percent of all gross revenues with expectations that the leaders and board members cannot have

salaries that are beyond market value set by the IRS. If the salaries are higher, they will be taxed separately at the standard individual rates.

This allows for social and local resources to be covered for nonprofit and religious groups.

What are your ideas for tax reform?

NOTES:

Conclusion

We have a host of different opinions regarding democracy. We may all be novices at understanding what is in the Constitution or the amendments. However, this is our chance to see what democracy is and what you believe needs to be changed.

There is space in this book to write down what you learn or what you believe needs changing in certain domains of our democracy. After you think about it, send your ideas to the blog **ctrl-alt-delete.us** and read what others think about this subject. I look forward to learning your opinions.

Appendix I

Government Documents

US Constitution—Original Transcript

(Wording and spelling may vary from this period of history).

https://www.archives.gov/founding-docs/constitution-transcript

We the People of the United States, in Order to form a more perfect Union, establish Justice, insure domestic Tranquility, provide for the common defence, promote the general Welfare, and secure the Blessings of Liberty to ourselves and our Posterity, do ordain and establish this Constitution for the United States of America.

Article. I.

Section. 1.

All legislative Powers herein granted shall be vested in a Congress of the United States, which shall consist of a Senate and House of Representatives.

Section. 2.

The House of Representatives shall be composed of Members chosen every second Year by the People of the several States, and the Electors in each State shall have the Qualifications requisite for Electors of the most numerous Branch of the State Legislature.

No Person shall be a Representative who shall not have attained to the Age of twenty five Years, and been seven Years a Citizen of the United States, and who shall not, when elected, be an Inhabitant of that State in which he shall be chosen.

Representatives and direct Taxes shall be apportioned among the several States which may be included within this Union, according to their respective Numbers, which shall be determined by adding to the whole Number of free Persons, including those bound to Service for a Term of Years, and excluding Indians not taxed, three fifths of all other Persons. The actual Enumeration shall be made within three Years after the first Meeting of the Congress of the United States, and within every subsequent Term of ten Years, in such

Manner as they shall by Law direct. The Number of Representatives shall not exceed one for every thirty Thousand, but each State shall have at Least one Representative; and until such enumeration shall be made, the State of New Hampshire shall be entitled to chuse three, Massachusetts eight, Rhode-Island and Providence Plantations one, Connecticut five, New-York six, New Jersey four, Pennsylvania eight, Delaware one, Maryland six, Virginia ten, North Carolina five, South Carolina five, and Georgia three.

When vacancies happen in the Representation from any State, the Executive Authority thereof shall issue Writs of Election to fill such Vacancies.

The House of Representatives shall chuse their Speaker and other Officers; and shall have the sole Power of Impeachment.

Section. 3.

The Senate of the United States shall be composed of two Senators from each State, chosen by the Legislature thereof, for six Years; and each Senator shall have one Vote.

Immediately after they shall be assembled in Consequence of the first Election, they shall be divided as equally as may be into three Classes. The Seats of the Senators of the first Class shall be vacated at the Expiration of the second Year, of the second

Class at the Expiration of the fourth Year, and of the third Class at the Expiration of the sixth Year, so that one third may be chosen every second Year; and if Vacancies happen by Resignation, or otherwise, during the Recess of the Legislature of any State, the Executive thereof may make temporary Appointments until the next Meeting of the Legislature, which shall then fill such Vacancies.

No Person shall be a Senator who shall not have attained to the Age of thirty Years, and been nine Years a Citizen of the United States, and who shall not, when elected, be an Inhabitant of that State for which he shall be chosen.

The Vice President of the United States shall be President of the Senate, but shall have no Vote, unless they be equally divided.

The Senate shall chuse their other Officers, and also a President pro tempore, in the Absence of the Vice President, or when he shall exercise the Office of President of the United States.

The Senate shall have the sole Power to try all Impeachments. When sitting for that Purpose, they shall be on Oath or Affirmation. When the President of the United States is tried, the Chief Justice shall preside: And no Person shall be convicted without the Concurrence of two thirds of the Members present.

Judgment in Cases of Impeachment shall not extend further than to removal from Office, and disqualification to hold and enjoy any Office of honor, Trust or Profit under the United States: but the Party convicted shall nevertheless be liable and subject to Indictment, Trial, Judgment and Punishment, according to Law.

Section. 4.

The Times, Places and Manner of holding Elections for Senators and Representatives, shall be prescribed in each State by the Legislature thereof; but the Congress may at any time by Law make or alter such Regulations, except as to the Places of chusing Senators.

The Congress shall assemble at least once in every Year, and such Meeting shall be on the first Monday in December, unless they shall by Law appoint a different Day.

Section. 5.

Each House shall be the Judge of the Elections, Returns and Qualifications of its own Members, and a Majority of each shall constitute a Quorum to do Business; but a smaller Number may adjourn from day to day, and may be authorized to compel the Attendance of absent Members, in such Manner, and under such Penalties as each House may provide.

Each House may determine the Rules of its Proceedings, punish its Members for disorderly Behaviour, and, with the Concurrence of two thirds, expel a Member.

Each House shall keep a Journal of its Proceedings, and from time to time publish the same, excepting such Parts as may in their Judgment require Secrecy; and the Yeas and Nays of the Members of either House on any question shall, at the Desire of one fifth of those Present, be entered on the Journal.

Neither House, during the Session of Congress, shall, without the Consent of the other, adjourn for more than three days, nor to any other Place than that in which the two Houses shall be sitting.

Section. 6.

The Senators and Representatives shall receive a Compensation for their Services, to be ascertained by Law, and paid out of the Treasury of the United States. They shall in all Cases, except Treason, Felony and Breach of the Peace, be privileged from Arrest during their Attendance at the Session of their respective Houses, and in going to and returning from the same; and for any Speech or Debate in either House, they shall not be questioned in any other Place.

No Senator or Representative shall, during the Time for which he was elected, be appointed to any civil Office under the Authority of the United States, which shall have been created, or the Emoluments whereof shall have been encreased during such time; and no Person holding any Office under the United States, shall be a Member of either House during his Continuance in Office.

Section. 7.

All Bills for raising Revenue shall originate in the House of Representatives; but the Senate may propose or concur with Amendments as on other Bills.

Every Bill which shall have passed the House of Representatives and the Senate, shall, before it become a Law, be presented to the President of the United States; If he approve he shall sign it, but if not he shall return it, with his Objections to that House in which it shall have originated, who shall enter the Objections at large on their Journal, and proceed to reconsider it. If after such Reconsideration two thirds of that House shall agree to pass the Bill, it shall be sent, together with the Objections, to the other House, by which it shall likewise be reconsidered, and if approved by two thirds of that House, it shall become a Law. But in all such Cases the Votes of both Houses shall be determined by yeas and Nays, and the Names of the Persons voting for and against the Bill shall be entered on the Journal of each House respectively. If any Bill shall not be returned by the President within ten Days (Sundays excepted) after it shall have been presented to him, the Same shall be a Law, in like Manner as if he had signed it, unless the Congress by their Adjournment prevent its Return, in which Case it shall not be a Law.

Every Order, Resolution, or Vote to which the Concurrence of the Senate and House of Representatives may be necessary (except on a question of Adjournment) shall be presented to the President of the United States; and before the Same shall take Effect, shall be approved by him, or being disapproved by him, shall be repassed by two thirds of the Senate and House of Representatives, according to the Rules and Limitations prescribed in the Case of a Bill.

Section. 8.

The Congress shall have Power To lay and collect Taxes, Duties, Imposts and Excises, to pay the Debts and provide for the common Defence and general Welfare of the United States; but all Duties, Imposts and Excises shall be uniform throughout the United States;

To borrow Money on the credit of the United States;

To regulate Commerce with foreign Nations, and among the several States, and with the Indian Tribes;

To establish an uniform Rule of Naturalization, and uniform Laws on the subject of Bankruptcies throughout the United States;

To coin Money, regulate the Value thereof, and of foreign Coin, and fix the Standard of Weights and Measures;

To provide for the Punishment of counterfeiting the Securities and current Coin of the United States;

To establish Post Offices and post Roads;

To promote the Progress of Science and useful Arts, by securing for limited Times to Authors and Inventors the exclusive Right to their respective Writings and Discoveries;

To constitute Tribunals inferior to the supreme Court;

To define and punish Piracies and Felonies committed on the high Seas, and Offences against the Law of Nations;

To declare War, grant Letters of Marque and Reprisal, and make Rules concerning Captures on Land and Water;

To raise and support Armies, but no Appropriation of Money to that Use shall be for a longer Term than two Years;

To provide and maintain a Navy;

To make Rules for the Government and Regulation of the land and naval Forces;

To provide for calling forth the Militia to execute the Laws of the Union, suppress Insurrections and repel Invasions;

To provide for organizing, arming, and disciplining, the Militia, and for governing such Part of them as may be employed in the Service of the United States, reserving to the States respectively, the Appointment of the Officers, and the Authority of training the Militia according to the discipline prescribed by Congress;

To exercise exclusive Legislation in all Cases whatsoever, over such District (not exceeding ten Miles square) as may, by Cession of particular States, and the Acceptance of Congress, become the Seat of the Government of the United States, and to exercise like Authority over all Places purchased by the Consent of the Legislature of the State in which the Same shall be, for the Erection of Forts, Magazines, Arsenals, dock-Yards, and other needful Buildings;—And

To make all Laws which shall be necessary and proper for carrying into Execution the foregoing Powers, and all other Powers vested by this Constitution in the Government of the United States, or in any Department or Officer thereof.

Section. 9.

The Migration or Importation of such Persons as any of the States now existing shall think proper to admit, shall not be prohibited by the Congress prior to the Year one thousand eight hundred and eight, but a Tax or duty may be imposed on such Importation, not exceeding ten dollars for each Person.

The Privilege of the Writ of Habeas Corpus shall not be suspended, unless when in Cases of Rebellion or Invasion the public Safety may require it.

No Bill of Attainder or ex post facto Law shall be passed.

No Capitation, or other direct, Tax shall be laid, unless in Proportion to the Census or enumeration herein before directed to be taken.

No Tax or Duty shall be laid on Articles exported from any State.

No Preference shall be given by any Regulation of Commerce or Revenue to the Ports of one State over those of another: nor shall Vessels bound to, or from, one State, be obliged to enter, clear, or pay Duties in another.

No Money shall be drawn from the Treasury, but in Consequence of Appropriations made by Law; and a regular Statement and Account of the Receipts and Expenditures of all public Money shall be published from time to time.

No Title of Nobility shall be granted by the United States: And no Person holding any Office of Profit or

Trust under them, shall, without the Consent of the Congress, accept of any present, Emolument, Office, or Title, of any kind whatever, from any King, Prince, or foreign State.

Section. 10.

No State shall enter into any Treaty, Alliance, or Confederation; grant Letters of Marque and Reprisal; coin Money; emit Bills of Credit; make any Thing but gold and silver Coin a Tender in Payment of Debts; pass any Bill of Attainder, ex post facto Law, or Law impairing the Obligation of Contracts, or grant any Title of Nobility.

No State shall, without the Consent of the Congress, lay any Imposts or Duties on Imports or Exports, except what may be absolutely necessary for executing it's inspection Laws: and the net Produce of all Duties and Imposts, laid by any State on Imports or Exports, shall be for the Use of the Treasury of the United States; and all such Laws shall be subject to the Revision and Controul of the Congress.

No State shall, without the Consent of Congress, lay any Duty of Tonnage, keep Troops, or Ships of War in time of Peace, enter into any Agreement or Compact with another State, or with a foreign Power, or engage in War, unless actually invaded, or in such imminent Danger as will not admit of delay.

Article. II.

Section. 1.

The executive Power shall be vested in a President of the United States of America. He shall hold his Office during the Term of four Years, and, together with the Vice President, chosen for the same Term, be elected, as follows

Each State shall appoint, in such Manner as the Legislature thereof may direct, a Number of Electors, equal to the whole Number of Senators and Representatives to which the State may be entitled in the Congress: but no Senator or Representative, or Person holding an Office of Trust or Profit under the United States, shall be appointed an Elector.

The Electors shall meet in their respective States, and vote by Ballot for two Persons, of whom one at least shall not be an Inhabitant of the same State with themselves. And they shall make a List of all the Persons voted for, and of the Number of Votes for each; which List they shall sign and certify, and transmit sealed to the Seat of the Government of the United States, directed to the President of the Senate. The President of the Senate shall, in the Presence of the Senate and House of Representatives, open all the Certificates, and the Votes shall then be counted. The Person having the greatest Number of Votes shall be the President, if such Number be a Majority of the whole Number of Electors appointed; and if there be more than one who have such Majority, and have an equal Number of Votes, then the House of Representatives shall immediately chuse by Ballot one of them for President; and if no Person have a Majority, then from the five highest on the List the said House shall in like Manner chuse the President. But in chusing the President, the Votes shall be taken by States, the Representation from each State having one Vote; A quorum for this Purpose shall consist of a Member or Members from two thirds of the States, and a Majority of all the States shall be necessary to a Choice. In every Case, after the Choice of the President, the Person having the greatest Number of Votes of the Electors shall be the Vice President. But if there should remain two or more who have equal Votes, the Senate shall chuse from them by Ballot the Vice President.

The Congress may determine the Time of chusing the Electors, and the Day on which they shall give their Votes; which Day shall be the same throughout the United States.

No Person except a natural born Citizen, or a Citizen of the United States, at the time of the Adoption of this Constitution, shall be eligible to the Office of President; neither shall any Person be eligible to that Office who shall not have attained to the Age of thirty five Years, and been fourteen Years a Resident within the United States.

In Case of the Removal of the President from Office, or of his Death, Resignation, or Inability to discharge the Powers and Duties of the said Office, the Same shall devolve on the Vice President, and the Congress may by Law provide for the Case of Removal, Death, Resignation or Inability, both of the President and Vice President, declaring what Officer shall then act as President, and such Officer shall act accordingly, until the Disability be removed, or a President shall be elected.

The President shall, at stated Times, receive for his Services, a Compensation, which shall neither be encreased nor diminished during the Period for which he shall have been elected, and he shall not receive within that Period any other Emolument from the United States, or any of them.

Before he enter on the Execution of his Office, he shall take the following Oath or Affirmation:—"I do solemnly swear (or affirm) that I will faithfully execute the Office of President of the United States, and will to the best of my Ability, preserve, protect and defend the Constitution of the United States."

Section. 2.

The President shall be Commander in Chief of the Army and Navy of the United States, and of the Militia of the several States, when called into the actual Service of the United States; he may require the Opinion, in writing, of the principal Officer in each of the executive Departments, upon any Subject relating to the Duties of their respective Offices, and he shall have Power to grant Reprieves and Pardons for Offences against the United States, except in Cases of Impeachment.

He shall have Power, by and with the Advice and Consent of the Senate, to make Treaties, provided two thirds of the Senators present concur; and he shall nominate, and by and with the Advice and Consent of the Senate, shall appoint Ambassadors, other public Ministers and Consuls, Judges of the supreme Court, and all other Officers of the United States, whose Appointments are not herein otherwise provided for, and which shall be established by Law: but the Congress may by Law vest the Appointment of such inferior Officers, as they think proper, in the President alone, in the Courts of Law, or in the Heads of Departments.

The President shall have Power to fill up all Vacancies that may happen during the Recess of the Senate, by granting Commissions which shall expire at the End of their next Session.

Section. 3.

He shall from time to time give to the Congress Information of the State of the Union, and recommend to their Consideration such Measures as he shall judge necessary and expedient; he may, on extraordinary

Occasions, convene both Houses, or either of them, and in Case of Disagreement between them, with Respect to the Time of Adjournment, he may adjourn them to such Time as he shall think proper; he shall receive Ambassadors and other public Ministers; he shall take Care that the Laws be faithfully executed, and shall Commission all the Officers of the United States.

Section. 4.

The President, Vice President and all civil Officers of the United States, shall be removed from Office on Impeachment for, and Conviction of, Treason, Bribery, or other high Crimes and Misdemeanors.

Article III.

Section. 1.

The judicial Power of the United States, shall be vested in one supreme Court, and in such inferior Courts as the Congress may from time to time ordain and establish. The Judges, both of the supreme and inferior Courts, shall hold their Offices during good Behaviour, and shall, at stated Times, receive for their Services, a Compensation, which shall not be diminished during their Continuance in Office.

Section. 2.

The judicial Power shall extend to all Cases, in Law and Equity, arising under this Constitution, the Laws of the United States, and Treaties made, or which shall be made, under their Authority;—to all Cases affecting Ambassadors, other public Ministers and Consuls;—to all Cases of admiralty and maritime Jurisdiction;—to Controversies to which the United States shall be a Party;—to Controversies between two or more States;— between a State and Citizens of another State,—between Citizens of different States,—between Citizens of the same State claiming Lands under Grants of different States, and between a State, or the Citizens thereof, and foreign States, Citizens or Subjects.

In all Cases affecting Ambassadors, other public Ministers and Consuls, and those in which a State shall be Party, the supreme Court shall have original Jurisdiction. In all the other Cases before mentioned, the supreme Court shall have appellate Jurisdiction, both as to Law and Fact, with such Exceptions, and under such Regulations as the Congress shall make.

The Trial of all Crimes, except in Cases of Impeachment, shall be by Jury; and such Trial shall be held in the State where the said Crimes shall have been committed; but when not committed within any State, the Trial shall be at such Place or Places as the Congress may by Law have directed.

Section. 3.

Treason against the United States, shall consist only in levying War against them, or in adhering to their

Enemies, giving them Aid and Comfort. No Person shall be convicted of Treason unless on the Testimony of two Witnesses to the same overt Act, or on Confession in open Court.

The Congress shall have Power to declare the Punishment of Treason, but no Attainder of Treason shall work Corruption of Blood, or Forfeiture except during the Life of the Person attainted.

Article. IV.

Section. 1.

Full Faith and Credit shall be given in each State to the public Acts, Records, and judicial Proceedings of every other State. And the Congress may by general Laws prescribe the Manner in which such Acts, Records and Proceedings shall be proved, and the Effect thereof.

Section. 2.

The Citizens of each State shall be entitled to all Privileges and Immunities of Citizens in the several States.

A Person charged in any State with Treason, Felony, or other Crime, who shall flee from Justice, and be found in another State, shall on Demand of the executive Authority of the State from which he fled, be delivered up, to be removed to the State having Jurisdiction of the Crime.

No Person held to Service or Labour in one State, under the Laws thereof, escaping into another, shall, in Consequence of any Law or Regulation therein, be discharged from such Service or Labour, but shall be delivered up on Claim of the Party to whom such Service or Labour may be due.

Section. 3.

New States may be admitted by the Congress into this Union; but no new State shall be formed or erected within the Jurisdiction of any other State; nor any State be formed by the Junction of two or more States, or Parts of States, without the Consent of the Legislatures of the States concerned as well as of the Congress.

The Congress shall have Power to dispose of and make all needful Rules and Regulations respecting the Territory or other Property belonging to the United States; and nothing in this Constitution shall be so construed as to Prejudice any Claims of the United States, or of any particular State.

Section. 4.

The United States shall guarantee to every State in this Union a Republican Form of Government, and shall protect each of them against Invasion; and on Application of the Legislature, or of the Executive (when the Legislature cannot be convened) against domestic Violence.

Article. V.

The Congress, whenever two thirds of both Houses shall deem it necessary, shall propose Amendments to this Constitution, or, on the Application of the Legislatures of two thirds of the several States, shall call a Convention for proposing Amendments, which, in either Case, shall be valid to all Intents and Purposes, as Part of this Constitution, when ratified by the Legislatures of three fourths of the several States, or by Conventions in three fourths thereof, as the one or the other Mode of Ratification may be proposed by the Congress; Provided that no Amendment which may be made prior to the Year One thousand eight hundred and eight shall in any Manner affect the first and fourth Clauses in the Ninth Section of the first Article; and that no State, without its Consent, shall be deprived of its equal Suffrage in the Senate.

Article. VI.

All Debts contracted and Engagements entered into, before the Adoption of this Constitution, shall be as valid against the United States under this Constitution, as under the Confederation.

This Constitution, and the Laws of the United States which shall be made in Pursuance thereof; and all Treaties made, or which shall be made, under the Authority of the United States, shall be the supreme Law of the Land; and the Judges in every State shall be bound thereby, any Thing in the Constitution or Laws of any State to the Contrary notwithstanding.

The Senators and Representatives before mentioned, and the Members of the several State Legislatures, and all executive and judicial Officers, both of the United States and of the several States, shall be bound by Oath or Affirmation, to support this Constitution; but no religious Test shall ever be required as a Qualification to any Office or public Trust under the United States.

Article. VII.

The Ratification of the Conventions of nine States, shall be sufficient for the Establishment of this Constitution between the States so ratifying the Same.

The Word, "the," being interlined between the seventh and eighth Lines of the first Page, The Word "Thirty" being partly written on an Erazure in the fifteenth Line of the first Page, The Words "is tried" being interlined between the thirty second and thirty third Lines of the first Page and the Word "the" being interlined between the forty third and forty fourth Lines of the second Page.

Attest William Jackson Secretary

done in Convention by the Unanimous Consent of the States present the Seventeenth Day of September in the Year of our Lord one thousand seven hundred and Eighty seven and of the Independance of the United

States of America the Twelfth In witness whereof We have hereunto subscribed our Names,

G°. Washington
President and deputy from Virginia

Summary of Constitutional Articles

https://www.archives.gov/founding-docs/constitution

The Constitution of the United States contains a preamble and seven articles that describe the way the government is structured and how it operates. The first three articles establish the three branches of government and their powers: Legislative (Congress), Executive (office of the President,) and Judicial (Federal court system). A system of checks and balances prevents any one of these separate powers from becoming dominant. Articles four through seven describe the relationship of the states to the Federal Government, establish the Constitution as the supreme law of the land, and define the amendment and ratification processes.

Article I assigns the responsibility for making laws to the Legislative Branch (Congress). Congress is divided into two parts, or "Houses," the House of Representatives and the Senate. The bicameral Congress was a compromise between the large states, which wanted representation based on population, and the small ones, which wanted the states to have equal representation.

Article II details the Executive Branch and the offices of the President and Vice President. It lays down rules for electing the President (through the Electoral College), eligibility (must be a natural-born citizen at least 35 years old), and term length. The 12th and 25th Amendments modified some of these rules.

Article III establishes the Judicial Branch with the U.S. Supreme Court as the federal court system's highest court. It specifies that Federal judges be appointed for life unless they commit a serious crime. This article is shorter than Articles I and II. The Federal Convention left much of the work of planning the court system to the First Congress. The 1789 Judiciary Act created the three-tiered court system in place today.

Article IV outlines states' powers in relationship to each other. States have the authority to create and enforce their own laws but must respect and help enforce the laws of other states. Congress may pass Federal laws regarding how states honor other states' laws and records.

Article V explains the amendment process, which is different and more difficult than the process for making laws. When two-thirds of the Senate and two-thirds of the House of Representatives vote to change the Constitution, an amendment goes to the state legislatures for a vote. Alternatively, two-thirds of the state legislatures can submit an application to Congress, and then Congress calls a national convention at which states propose amendments. Three-fourths of the state legislatures or state conventions must vote in favor of an amendment to ratify it.

Article VI states that Federal law is supreme, or higher than, state and local laws. This means that if a state law conflicts with a Federal law, Federal law takes precedence.

Article VII describes the ratification process for the Constitution. It called for special state ratifying conventions. Nine states were required to enact the Constitution. Rhode Island became the 13th state to ratify the Constitution in 1790.

Appendix II

Amendments to the Constitution—Open Source

https://www.govinfo.gov/content/pkg/GPO-CONAN-1992/pdf/GPO-CONAN-1992-7.pdf

ARTICLES IN ADDITION TO, AND AMENDMENT OF, THE CONSTITUTION OF THE UNITED STATES OF AMERICA, PROPOSED BY CONGRESS, AND RATIFIED BY THE SEVERAL STATES, PURSUANT TO THE FIFTH ARTICLE OF THE ORIGINAL CONSTITUTION

AMENDMENT [I.] Congress shall make no law respecting an establishment of religion, or prohibiting the free exercise thereof; or abridging the freedom of speech, or of the press; or the right of the people peaceably to assemble, and to petition the Government for a redress of grievances.

AMENDMENT [II.] A well regulated Militia, being necessary to the security of a free State, the right of the people to keep and bear Arms, shall not be infringed.

AMENDMENT [III.] No Soldier shall, in time of peace be quartered in any house, without the consent of the Owner, nor in time of war, but in a manner to be prescribed by law.

AMENDMENT [IV.] The right of the people to be secure in their persons, houses, papers, and effects, against unreasonable searches and seizures, shall not be violated, and no Warrants shall issue, but upon probable cause, supported by Oath or affirmation, and particularly describing the place to be searched, and the persons or things to be seized.

AMENDMENT [V.] No person shall be held to answer for a capital, or otherwise infamous crime, unless on a presentment or indictment of a Grand Jury, except in cases arising in the land or naval forces, or in the Militia, when in actual service in time of War or public danger; nor shall any person be subject for the same offence to be twice put in jeopardy of life or limb; nor shall be compelled in any criminal case to be a witness against himself, nor be deprived of life, liberty, or property, without due process of law; nor shall private property be taken for public use, without just compensation.

AMENDMENT [VI.] In all criminal prosecutions, the accused shall enjoy the right to a speedy and public trial, by an impartial jury of the State and district wherein the crime shall have been committed, which district shall have been previously ascertained by law, and to be informed of the nature and cause of the accusation; to be confronted with the witnesses against him; to have compulsory process for obtaining witnesses in his favor, and to have the Assistance of Counsel for his defense.

AMENDMENT [VII.] In Suits at common law, where the value in controversy shall exceed twenty dollars, the right of trial by jury shall be preserved, and no fact tried by a jury, shall be otherwise re-examined in any Court of the United States, than according to the rules of the common law.

AMENDMENT [VIII.] Excessive bail shall not be required, nor excessive fines imposed, nor cruel and unusual punishments inflicted.

AMENDMENT [IX.] The enumeration in the Constitution, of certain rights, shall not be construed to deny or disparage others retained by the people.

AMENDMENT [X.] The powers not delegated to the United States by the Constitution, nor prohibited by it to the States, are reserved to the States respectively, or to the people.

AMENDMENT [XI.] The Judicial power of the United States shall not be construed to extend to any suit in law or equity, commenced or prosecuted against one on the United States by Citizens of another State, or by Citizens or Subjects of any Foreign State.

AMENDMENT [XII.] The Electors shall meet in their respective states and vote by ballot for President and Vice-President, one of whom, at least, shall not be an inhabitant of the same state with themselves; they shall name in their ballots the person voted for as President, and in distinct ballots the person voted for as VicePresident, and they shall make distinct lists of all persons voted for as President, and of all persons voted for as VicePresident, and of the number of votes for each, which lists they shall sign and certify, and transmit sealed to the seat of the government of the United States, directed to the President of the Senate;—The President of the Senate shall, in the presence of the Senate and House of Representatives, open all the certificates and the votes shall then be counted;—The person having the greatest Number of votes for President, shall be the President, if such number be a majority of the whole number of Electors appointed; and if no person have such majority, then from the persons having the highest numbers not exceeding three on the list of those voted for as President, the House of Representatives shall choose immediately, by ballot, the President. But in choosing the President, the votes shall be taken by states, the representation from each state having one vote; a quorum for this purpose shall consist of a member or members from two-thirds of the states, and a majority of all the states shall be necessary to a choice. And if the House of Representatives shall not choose a President whenever the right of choice shall devolve upon them, before the fourth day of March next following, then the Vice-President shall act as President, as in the case of the death or other constitutional disability of the President—The person having the greatest number of votes as Vice-President, shall be the Vice-President, if such number be a majority of the whole number of Electors appointed, and if no person have a majority, then from the two highest numbers on the list, the Senate shall choose the Vice-President; a quorum for the purpose shall consist of two-thirds of the whole number of Senators, and a majority of the whole number shall be necessary to a choice. But no person constitutionally ineligible to the office of President shall be eligible to that of Vice President of the United States.

AMENDMENT XIII.

SECTION 1. Neither slavery nor involuntary servitude, except as a punishment for crime whereof the party shall have been duly convicted, shall exist within the United States, or any place subject to their jurisdiction.

SECTION 2. Congress shall have power to enforce this article by appropriate legislation.

AMENDMENT XIV.

SECTION. 1. All persons born or naturalized in the United States and subject to the jurisdiction thereof, are citizens of the United States and of the State wherein they reside. No State shall make or enforce any law which shall abridge the privileges or immunities of citizens of the United States; nor shall any State deprive any person of life, liberty, or property, without due process of law; nor deny to any person within its jurisdiction the equal protection of the laws.

SECTION. 2. Representatives shall be apportioned among the several States according to their respective numbers, counting the whole number of persons in each State, excluding Indians not taxed. But when the right to vote at any election for the choice of electors for President and Vice President of the United States, Representatives in Congress, the Executive and Judicial officers of a State, or the members of the Legislature thereof, is denied to any of the male inhabitants of such State, being twenty-one years of age, and citizens of the United States, or in any way abridged, except for participation in rebellion, or other crime, the basis of representation therein shall be reduced in the proportion which the number of such male citizens shall bear to the whole number of male citizens twenty-one years of age in such State.

SECTION. 3. No person shall be a Senator or Representative in Congress, or elector of President and Vice President, or hold any office, civil or military, under the United States, or under any State, who, having previously taken an oath, as a member of Congress, or as an officer of the United States, or as a member of any State legislature, or as an executive or judicial officer of any State, to support the Constitution of the United States, shall have engaged in insurrection or rebellion against the same, or given aid or comfort to the enemies thereof. But Congress may by a vote of two-thirds of each House, remove such disability.

SECTION. 4. The validity of the public debt of the United States, authorized by law, including debts incurred for payment of pensions and bounties for services in suppressing insurrection or rebellion, shall not be questioned. But neither the United States nor any State shall assume or pay any debt or obligation incurred in aid of insurrection or rebellion against the United States, or any claim for the loss or emancipation of any slave; but all such debts, obligations and claims shall be held illegal and void.

SECTION. 5. The Congress shall have power to enforce, by appropriate legislation, the provisions of this article.

AMENDMENT XV.

SECTION. 1. The right of citizens of the United States to vote shall not be denied or abridged by the United States or by any State on account of race, color, or previous condition of servitude.

SECTION. 2. The Congress shall have power to enforce this article by appropriate legislation.

AMENDMENT XVI. The Congress shall have power to lay and collect taxes on incomes, from whatever source derived, without apportionment among the several States, and without regard to any census or enumeration.

AMENDMENT [XVII.] The Senate of the United States shall be composed of two Senators from each State, elected by the people thereof, for six years; and each Senator shall have one vote. The electors in each State shall have the qualifications requisite for electors of the most numerous branch of the State legislatures. When vacancies happen in the representation of any State in the Senate, the executive authority of such State shall issue writs of election to fill such vacancies: Provided, That the legislature of any State may empower the executive thereof to make temporary appointments until the people fill the vacancies by election as the legislature may direct. This amendment shall not be so construed as to affect the election or term of any Senator chosen before it becomes valid as part of the Constitution.

AMENDMENT [XVIII.]

SECTION. 1. After one year from the ratification of this article the manufacture, sale, or transportation of intoxicating liquors within, the importation thereof into, or the exportation thereof from the United States and all territory subject to the jurisdiction thereof for beverage purposes is hereby prohibited.

SECTION. 2. The Congress and the several States shall have concurrent power to enforce this article by appropriate legislation.

SECTION. 3. This article shall be inoperative unless it shall have been ratified as an amendment to the Constitution by the legislatures of the several States, as provided in the Constitution, within seven years from the date of the submission hereof to the States by the Congress.

AMENDMENT [XIX.] The right of citizens of the United States to vote shall not be denied or abridged by the United States or by any State on account of sex. Congress shall have power to enforce this article by appropriate legislation.

AMENDMENT [XX.]

SECTION. 1. The terms of the President and Vice President shall end at noon on the 20th day of January, and the terms of Senators and Representatives at noon on the 3d day of January, of the years in which such terms would have ended if this article had not been ratified; and the terms of their successors shall then begin.

SECTION. 2. The Congress shall assemble at least once in every year, and such meeting shall begin at noon on the 3d day of January, unless they shall by law appoint a different day.

SECTION. 3. If, at the time fixed for the beginning of the term of the President, the President elect shall have died, the Vice President elect shall become President. If a President shall not have been chosen before the time fixed for the beginning of his term, or if the President elect shall have failed to qualify, then the Vice President elect shall act as President until a President shall have qualified; and the Congress may by law provide for the case wherein neither a President elect nor a Vice President elect shall have qualified, declaring who shall then act as President, or the manner in which one who is to act shall be selected, and such person shall act accordingly until a President or Vice President shall have qualified.

SECTION. 4. The Congress may by law provide for the case of the death of any of the persons from whom the House of Representatives may choose a President whenever the right of choice shall have devolved upon them, and for the case of the death of any of the persons from whom the Senate may choose a Vice President whenever the right of choice shall have devolved upon them.

SECTION. 5. Sections 1 and 2 shall take effect on the 15th day of October following the ratification of this article.

SECTION. 6. This article shall be inoperative unless it shall have been ratified as an amendment to the Constitution by the legislatures of three-fourths of the several States within seven years from the date of its submission.

AMENDMENT [XXI.]

SECTION. 1. The eighteenth article of amendment to the Constitution of the United States is hereby repealed.

SECTION. 2. The transportation or importation into any State, Territory, or possession of the United States for delivery or use therein of intoxicating liquors, in violation of the laws thereof, is hereby prohibited.

SECTION. 3. This article shall be inoperative unless it shall have been ratified as an amendment to the Constitution by conventions in the several States, as provided in the Constitution, within seven years from the date of the submission hereof to the States by the Congress.

AMENDMENT [XXII.]

SECTION. 1. No person shall be elected to the office of the President more than twice, and no person who has held the office of President, or acted as President, for more than two years of a term to which some other person was elected President shall be elected to the office of the President more than once. But this Article shall not apply to any person holding the office of President, when this Article was proposed by the Congress, and shall not prevent any person who may be holding the office of President, or acting as President, during the term within which this Article becomes operative from holding the office of President or acting as President during the remainder of such term.

SECTION. 2. This article shall be inoperative unless it shall have been ratified as an amendment to the Constitution by the legislatures of three-fourths of the several States within seven years from the date of its submission to the States by the Congress.

AMENDMENT [XXIII.]

SECTION. 1. The District constituting the seat of Government of the United States shall appoint in such manner as the Congress may direct: A number of electors of President and Vice President equal to the whole number of Senators and Representatives in Congress to which the District would be entitled if it were a State, but in no event more than the least populous State; they shall be in addition to those appointed by the States, but they shall be considered, for the purposes of the election of President and Vice President, to be electors appointed by a State; and they shall meet in the District and perform such duties as provided by the twelfth article of amendment.

SECTION. 2. The Congress shall have power to enforce this article by appropriate legislation.

AMENDMENT [XXIV.]

SECTION. 1. The right of citizens of the United States to vote in any primary or other election for President or Vice President, for electors for President or Vice President, or for Senator or Representative in Congress, shall not be denied or abridged by the United States or any State by reason of failure to pay any poll tax or other tax.

SECTION. 2. The Congress shall have power to enforce this article by appropriate legislation.

AMENDMENT [XXV.]

SECTION. 1. In case of the removal of the President from office or of his death or resignation, the Vice President shall become President.

SECTION. 2. Whenever there is a vacancy in the office of the Vice President, the President shall nominate a Vice President who shall take office upon confirmation by a majority vote of both Houses of Congress.

SECTION. 3. Whenever the President transmits to the President pro tempore of the Senate and the Speaker of the House of Representatives has written declaration that he is unable to discharge the powers and duties of his office, and until he transmits to them a written declaration to the contrary, such powers and duties shall be discharged by the Vice President as Acting President.

SECTION. 4. Whenever the Vice President and a majority of either the principal officers of the executive departments or of such other body as Congress may by law provide, transmit to the President pro tempore of the Senate and the Speaker of the House of Representatives their written declaration that the President is unable to discharge the powers and duties of his office, the Vice President shall immediately assume the powers and duties of the office as Acting President. Thereafter, when the President transmits to the President pro tempore of the Senate and the Speaker of the House of Representatives has written declaration that no inability exists, he shall resume the powers and duties of his office unless the Vice President and a majority of either the principal officers of the executive department or of such other body as Congress may by law provide, transmit within four days to the President pro tempore of the Senate and the Speaker of the House of Representatives their written declaration that the President is unable to discharge the powers and duties of his office. Thereupon Congress shall decide the issue, assembling within forty-eight hours for that purpose if not in session. If the Congress, within twenty-one days after receipt of the latter written declaration, or, if Congress is not in session, within twenty-one days after Congress is required to assemble, determines by two-thirds vote of both Houses that the President is unable to discharge the powers and duties of his office, the Vice President shall continue to discharge the same as Acting President; otherwise, the President shall resume the powers and duties of his office.

AMENDMENT [XXVI]

SECTION. 1. The right of citizens of the United States, who are eighteen years of age or older, to vote shall not be denied or abridged by the United States or by any State on account of age.

SECTION. 2. The Congress shall have power to enforce this article by appropriate legislation.

AMENDMENT [XXVII] No law varying the compensation for the services of the Senators and Representatives shall take effect, until an election of Representatives shall have intervened.

Made in the USA
Las Vegas, NV
04 September 2021